Near Truth Only

Ed Higgins

Fernwood
PRESS

Near Truth Only

Fernwood Press
Newberg, Oregon
www.fernwoodpress.com

Printed in the United States of America

Cover and interior design: Mareesa Fawver Moss
Cover photo: James Wainscoat

ISBN 978-1-59498-094-7

for Tricia—

the gift you are:
Healer
Sharer
Sure Love

Contents

These poems first appeared in the following publications:

"Syntax Connections" in *Haibun Today*; "Storytelling" in *Concho River Review*; "Grunion Fishing" in *Peacock Journal*; "Astrobiography" in *Point Mass Anthology*; "He drank" in *Haibun Today*; "the full moon's light" in *The BeZine*; "Outside" in *qarrtsiluni online literary magazine*; "Ok, ok, so I concede" in *Shot Glass Journal*; "Kitchen Fruit Fly Suicides" in *Triggerfish Critical Review*; "Anticipating Winter" in *The Plum Tree Tavern*; "We two" in *Blue Heron Review*; "The looking glass predator" in *Triggerfish Critical Review*; "When the wind/sky really is God" in *The Windhover*; "Without Knowing It" in *The Merton Seasonal: A Quarterly Review*; "Remembering Eden" in *Vita Brevis Press*; "Via Dolorosa" in *Embers Igniting*; "Sappho" in *The Ekphrastic Review*; "Tohono O'odham: The Desert People" in *Line Rider Press*; "Side by Each" in *Nightingale & Sparrow*.

I.

I

Syntax Connections

Consider this. Only a sentence ago we were complete strangers,
oceans of time, distance, and thought between us. Once inside,
the written word has such beguiling power. Like moon-tide, some
sheer magic drew us into these unfolding words, their perfect
syntax of word on word, sentence upon sentence, whole thoughts
connecting between us. As in the chambered nautilus whose
spiraled pearlescent luster holds a geometry belonging only there.
Likewise, we spiral through words searching some new treasure,
exploring deep nuanced word-rooms, believing some meaning
more than the ocean's dark sound can be found there.

Storytelling

We all tell them,
even when our mothers
warned us only the Devil
tells stories, and the truth
is best in all situations,
will always protect us
in the end. The end in those days
being usually at the end of her
patience. Still, I began to notice,
if you were to be fully loved,
a certain amount of storytelling
was absolutely necessary. Like the
time burglars broke into my bedroom
and peed in my bed to my blameless
horror. *And apparently peed too in your
pajamas*, pointed out my mother.
Yes, I quickly revised my story,
they made me take off my pajamas
to search for hidden gold and jewels,
and when they didn't find any,
they got angry and also peed on my PJ's.
Needless to say, my mother laughed
at this well-crafted story. Which made me forever
see the value of focused revision. Especially
in a story laced with any kind of potential
tragedy. For I then told her they wanted
to kidnap me for ransom but decided
in the end because I was loved so much
this would be a crime for which
they could never be forgiven.
I have since told stories even to the Devil
on occasion, and while actually few have
been accounted as truth by him,
he has been so tickled by my honed
inventions, he shakes with laughter every time.

Grunion Fishing

*"Of course, most of the things I look back on fondly I never actually
experienced."*
—Jon Favreau

As spilled on a sandy Corona del Mar beach
both in moonlight and starlight so lovely
and strangely sad as if receding still
on the waves there in lost time or no time at all
except for nostalgia now, or as it actually happened maybe
those flickerings of pale silver on thousands of grunion
making the whole surf-pounded beach alive
with the magic incandescence of slender wriggling fish.

And we two once waiting under bluish moonlight at high tide
that long summer's night ago while giddy in the crashing waves
with scooping up whole handfuls of slippery small fish
into buckets bright with overflowing moon.

Using flashlights so as not to scare the fish
watching the female arching her body
as her tail sinks deep into the fluid sand
while the male curls around her
milt flowing down her silvery sides and belly
fertilizing buried eggs beneath.

Then later wrapped in one another's arms
listening to the sound of ourselves
pounding in our veins as the waves recede.

Overwhelmed ever after by the ability to catch
starlight's incandescence ourselves:
far-traveling light and flecks of photon stars
which must stay momentarily or even forever in the mind.

All beneath the spawning of that bright above us night sky
on a warm California beach.

Astrobiography

I have this friend in science
who tells me how he learned
astrophysics. It goes something
like this: You first lean so closely into
the source of things that
distant stars, whole galaxies,
collapse as if into the eye
of a great storm called God.
And what is important then
is how long you can hold your own
eye open to the center of mystery—
which is your lens—
as if you'd just discovered
some incomprehensible
petroglyph in a dark cave
somewhere under France maybe
only you have no light
but your own imagination
and the ocean called language.
Then as if the universe itself
were lethal oxygen,
you breathe wonder in
slowly

at the speed of lightheadedness.

He drank

excessively. And this worried her, of course. But in WWII, he'd
been a tail gunner in a B17 Flying Fortress. He completed seven
sorties over German-occupied Europe. Over France he was shot
down and declared missing in action, presumed dead. She spent
most of the government insurance money, then moved in with
her parents in Bangor with her two young children.

> noon's summer sun
> line-dried towels
> rubbing her shoulders

He had been wounded earlier in a Bremen raid, struck by flak
twice in his right leg. So he had bad dreams when he came back
from the dead. With shrapnel now in his back also, from German
Focke-Wulf 190 fighters that shot down his Flying Fortress,
shooting parachuting crew members as they drifted down over
French hayfields. He also beat her up occasionally when drunk.

> all these wars
> both inside and out
> the shifted earth

Mostly nothing terribly serious, some bruises, a black eye now and
then. Once matted blood in her hair from a large cut when he
shoved her against the door frame as she was coming out of the
locked bathroom where she'd retreated to escape his rage. She
thought he was gone, but he had silently waited in the hallway
for her to come out. When he grabbed her, she fell backward
cracking her head sharply against the door moulding's edge. Her
crying and the blood stopped his anger as he helped her up and
back into the bathroom, daubing the bleeding gash himself with
a wet washcloth, repeating how sorry he was. She forgave him.
The seven stitches left a scar and a slight bald spot.

All scars are areas of fibrous tissue, replacing normal skin after injury or disease, and have inferior functional quality.

remembering once
she spent the night
crying in his arms

the full moon's light

in warrior eyes
against life's flow

the AK47's steel kiss
the barrel's small o

concentrated in leaden thought

in the chamber nests
a fertilized zygote

snug in its brass case womb

all this dying war
both inside and outside:

wash away this death—
it clings to my bones

Outside

It's one of those days
when the cold, fog-dented sky
won't let you see even down
to the barn from the house.

On days like this
the silvered gray air
sticks in your lungs
like campfire marshmallows.

The cold of it slicks off
your fingernails. And the cows
in the barn loafing area
are hunched nearly into the letter C.

Only the Indian Runner ducks seem
to welcome this damp air
eating cracked corn and sunflower seeds
washed down by gulps of fog.

Ok, ok, so I concede

some answers are enough to make you cry or laugh yourself to death.
Funny to think we can see all the way past the sky and stars
sometimes, even to the ocean floor if we dive deep enough. But
yet just between
you
and
me
and
another
glass
of your favorite dark wine,
we are all on a trembling shore strolling along a minor cosmic beach
somewhere in the Milky Way's stellar fog holding hands with God
maybe making love-not-war or both sometimes within our bungeed
contingency. Or at least listening to gulls and the milk-white
breakers shifting sands of quandary watching at the edge of silences,
mystery twinkling light-years out towards countless
galactic clusters.

Wolf Spiders in My Kitchen Sink

Many bleary mornings stumbling from bed,
desperate to reach the coffeepot,
I'm startled by a wolf spider in the kitchen sink,
guarding one of its corners

sometimes hidden under the edge of an
unwashed dinner plate. I always check those
plate edges since my wife washes any discovered
wolf spider down the drain in a flush of cold water.

I keep a small Dixie cup within sideboard reach.
Usually spiders can be scooped easily in—but not always.
With Ferrari-like speed they can panic, eight-leg-it
to a farther corner. But they cannot escape for long.

On a second or third try, with cautious finger persuasion,
I pop them into the Dixie cup. Moving to the back door,
I flip the cup upside down, and the wolf spider joins
whatever backyard-freedom offers.

I wish them well. But I've read wolf spiders are master predators,
so I'd rather not have one in my bleary-eyed morning sink—
yet another example of irrational human reasoning.
Recently three wolf spiders were lurking!

The smallest of them looked understandably concerned.
Nor could I blame its nervous glances, so I rescued that one first.

Kitchen Fruit Fly Suicides

How the hell do these
1/8-inch-long
red-eyed flying insects
wind up in my kitchen
anyway? And why
are they forever committing
suicide in the glass of wine
I'm sipping while preparing dinner?

Sometimes I delicately teaspoon
out three or four drowned floaters,
losing the barest bit
of my supper-prep indulgence
before taking another sip
of a favorite pinot.

But only if I remember to look for
their floating specks
in my irresistible volatile lake.
The little winged bastards come
swarming from the kiwi fruit
over-ripening on the window shelf
above the kitchen counter.

Or from hovering like nano-drones
above the banana, clementine,
and apple fruit basket sitting
on the Hoosier cabinet's slide-out shelf.
Sometimes I just say
to-hell-with-you at drunken or dead
drosophila floating in my wine.

By now they're just wine-soaked
protein after all. It's bottom's up
on these suicide-prone fermented
fruit connoisseurs. Especially
if I'm on my second or third glass
of that fermented fruit.

Anticipating Winter

Today there are definite signs:

gray sky and clouds
their core dark as sorrow

torrent rain driven aslant
against the barn's side

swollen Yamhill Creek
furious with water

another V of geese
over the farm this morning

the plowed field soggy underfoot
fixed on distant May

a hawk hung in chill October air
like a narrow-winged thought.

We two

have this entire lifetime left, so let's waste it
still in whatever repair we can manage. I'll
bury my face in your still beautiful hair, breathing
in all our forgotten and remembered treasures,
the gray-streaked years melting like a Dalí clock.
We ripen in time like fall colors of the tall liquid
amber we planted beyond the pump house years
ago. Our mixed pulse an extravagant music of
complexities, joy and grief, while we pause here
on this moonless night listening in one another's
arms, embracing all those lost ghosts, waiting for
others to arrive, bound to their voices catching at
the soul's happy or sad fire. Love's the surest sign
you say, and I agree, its absence or loss a sure proof.

The Looking Glass Predator

In the mirror an owl staring you in the face once again,
a fraught fragment of life's puzzle. But you pretend it's

a lesser predator, maybe some buzzard doppelgänger
looking out. Not remembering they go first for the eyes,

eating until they reach your immortal or mortal soul,
whichever it is. Or maybe instead you want a liver-eating

eagle feasting steadfastly on your then regenerated fears
and failings. Better yet, make it the extinct Kelenken,

its massive beak shattering your ever-shifting self. Emitting
from the staring-back mirror some kind of predator truthfulness

which like the more staid mirror-staring owl keeps asking
whoo-whoo-who-the-hell are you anyway?

Dicing Onions

I'm in the kitchen, too damn hurried. Inattentive
at dicing onions while listening to Rod Stewart's
"The First Cut Is the Deepest," the song's irony

or onion-induced tears obscuring my vision. Tears,
as often, a recognition of our frequently delicate life,
as in Stewart's plea: "Just help me dry the tears that I've cried."

And that, just as I've run my finger under the knife's keen edge!
A rash jolt into one's knowledge of flesh's weakness,
alerting to life's obvious ability to cause pain, to draw blood,

those punishing wounds cutting to the bone. When you then realize
life's become a diced onion while you were otherwise distracted,
offering excruciating venom, as in the hidden spur of the male platypus.

At my cutting board, warm blood pools off my finger, dripping
into the partly diced onion with a strange mixed-color beauty
I'm oddly serene to accept, as tranquilly as if the blood of Christ

is casting forgiveness over my harried meal preparation. Now become
a kind of blood-Eucharist, as I halt before the bathroom's medicine cabinet
to seal away the brightness of my carelessly flowing blood.

II.

II

Transitions

When the moon scrapes past obscuring clouds,
there is the startle of pale-yellow light
escaping the sky onto the pasture, where
I walk my two young whippets in early spring
listening to chorus frogs shamelessly seeking
mates in the marsh-ponds spring rain has become
in my back pasture. And then coyotes too on the
far hill startling the dogs with their turbulent yips
joining the necessary summoning for more
of this tipping into spring, night-ascending prayers to
the moon and watching stars. But the moonlight's
caught sounds of fecundity are deceiving—cold north wind
needles my cheeks, embraces my earlobes despite the
upturned hood on my too-thin jacket. A light frost
on pasture-grass licks against my winter chore boots. Despite the
whetted signs and sounds of approaching spring, there is
yet to be early crocus, daffodils filling the yard, or leaves
on the maple trees that will later shade the pigs in summer
now shivering in the night's transition in the barnyard.

When the wind/sky really is God

and all the trees are holding
their limbs up in prayer

and rain is mating with soil
and loam itself is sperm

life for the oak or maple
or any other tree

and you stand there admiring
the green or red or orange

or brown leaves depending on
the season's fecundity

or maybe just enjoying
the stark-naked tree in winter

and the whole thing is a gift
to the wind/sky God

or to whatever is beyond the sky
where solar winds that are now swirling

stream out into the infinite universe
which is hope or at least something like it

looping back toward us at the speed of prayer
where it helps keep pace with dreams

that can eventually outdistance even
those forms of darkness at the center

of nearly everyone's need for
forgetting and forgiveness.

Without Knowing It

"We are full of paradise without knowing it."
—Thomas Merton

If this isn't Paradise, what is?
Your own eyes wide with
the imagination, the knowing,
the not-knowing of it all.

As the sometimes porcelain
of summer clouds, or
their crow's-wing black
of threatening, then actual, rain.

Or as in your vegetable garden,
tomatoes so near to ripe
you can't wait to pick them.
But must, knowing the
ripe taste worth the mid-July wait.

And then there is garden corn,
almost Heaven itself (even if
not a worshipper of Centeōtl,
the Aztec maize god) slathered
with butter, salt, and pepper.

Everything alive or dead, or
whatever's in between, as
most things are. As our rapt
or frightened attention
to contingency demands.

Or else just to prove you're
able to stand it all sometimes.
Then you can at least pretend
it's all meaningful. And maybe it is.

Eve waking

near the one tree
his miraculous voice
whispered like scented
garden air

as against her
he twined and reached
caressing earth-brown hair

the tree remembers:
two entwined
all the moon bright night
they coiled and shuddered
on the fallen leaves there

he nearly forgetting
the blasphemous dawn
beside her sweet fright
on the spent ground

the left-behind core
and ripe Eve
the half-eaten fruit
sacred, bitter seed

enfleshed woman
waking full of desire
knowing now
the double pain she must bear.

Remembering Eden

Lying in clover and brome
eye against the sky
that never blinks,

although daily closes,

distant smoke wisps
above the chimney
drifting over wild lupine:

prayer's hopeful rise
heavenward.
Eve there with child again
pouring ash in boiling lard
to scrub and clean away

dark earth's laboring stain.

Tall poplars we first planted
shadow the late summer's
afternoon sun—

on the house I will die in.

Icon: Christ of Sinai

Directly in front of me
he is here,
him on this quiet morning
in a room of the Byzantine Museum, Athens,
in the hundred-degree heat and dust
of a city not yet fully awake.
Here, and I am suddenly confronted—
the oldest icon in existence—with
his image.

The rest of the room evaporates,
and all I see is him:
Pure mystery, great and wondrous,
dizzying and terrible.

How can wood and pigment
egg yolk and animal skin convey
such ethereal truth,
intensify the power,
captivate Christian eye and heart?

Christ of Sinai looks at me
with steady gaze.
His eyes—the famed twins
Justice and Mercy—
see straight through me
piercing the whitewashed tomb
of my exterior till it hurts.
One eye is dark, foreboding
shadows between the brow and lid
deepening and on the verge of righteous anger—
the other eye embraces all
even my unworthy soul.
I stand and cannot pray. My eyes swell with tears.
I cannot look anymore.

It is the eyes, dark and arresting,
sometimes frightening,
that call out to the viewer.
Eyes painted in encaustic technique
using beeswax mixed with pigment
applied in pure form while hot.
The iconographer fasts and prays while painting,
saturating every brushstroke with intercessions.

Even robbers could not bear to look
into the power of this presence.
It was the eyes of icons Turkish warriors
scratched out when pillaging
the monasteries of Greece.

Silent Prayer

At this moment
there are struggles

beyond these words
to write down,

images that scheme
or dream unable

to become wisdom
or even travail

in this mute present
where I endure truth's

anxious paradox.
Past this false self

I can never wholly claim.

Let my words be few,
renew the silence itself

that was not shattered
nor enough.

Of Light

"Believing in the Light you shall not abide in darkness."
—George Fox (1654)

Light's labor
is to tell darkness back,
push it toward eternity's edge—

although much darkness slips back
through, grieving the hearts
of all who must live here.

Like lead, darkness weighs
nearly as much as gold.

But Light's feel
is the alchemy of love
falling in bright color,

as stars sometimes do,
back to earth's gravity.

There, turned to chemical
(even among fireflies)
it burns gold-like

attracting more love still
across open hearts,

against night's threshold.

Peoplewalk Tunnel

At step-blinding speed we alight everywhere, more
than occasionally to laugh at ourselves, as well as at our
whole burlesque human race, hopefully with some relieving hope.

Although pouring down tears too. Otherwise scorpions
the size of hate or worry can plunge venom into our primitive lizard
brains, where it sputters baneful toxin stimuli, passing into

our medulla autonomic thoughts and impulse actions
without sufficient consideration. Not unlike those distracting
flashing neon lights overhead at O'Hare's B and C connecting concourse.

The pulsing neon rainbow runs the corridor's ceiling length
along with synchronized music distraction. Then a mechanical
prophet-voice at the end of the peoplewalk gives laconic warning:

Look down, look down, look down! Everybody needs to watch
their step because our burlesque journey is always abruptly ending.

Via Dolorosa

God dying
   the paradox
   harder than Hell
   to understand

Judean dust
   was real enough though
   and taut crowds in
   angry afternoon sun

their faces
   blurred by stumbling pain
   of blood/sweat back
   and thorn/torn brow

and dark spatters
   like wine-red coins
   fell to that road
   anointing our way

poem for mary

that seed
being no abstract
notion
grew in secret
a while
until those
forming curves
pushed into
shameful
recognition

whispers grew
then, too,
at these
(some thought)
clear signs

but you knew
beyond their
doubt
those life signs
within

that god-gift
foretold
bethlehem's
night blaze
of promise

seeing all
our darkness
ended

Sappho

Two Roman busts have come down to us, both copies
of supposed earlier Greek originals, from the 4th century BC.

One has two long stylized hair locks flowing down
the bust's front to where her breasts would be if the modest

marble had presented us with such. Her locks flow
as multiple stylized curls, crescent-like across her forehead.

The second Roman bust, from another lost Hellenistic original,
shows Sappho with shorter hair tucked under some kind

of band around her forehead—while slipping beneath the band,
short, slightly curly hair runs along the sides, revealing her ears.

Her lips are fuller here and the nose prominently Roman,
which has suffered some kind of desecration or damage.

Her eyes and slightly tilted head seem pleading
or perhaps only in pondering thought.

An early depiction of Sappho also survives on an Attic red-figure
kalathos, a kind of ceramic vase in the shape of a household basket.

Here she is holding a plectrum and lyre while turning to listen
to her contemporary poet-friend Alcaeus, also holding a lyre.

Another Greek pottery vessel, used for carrying water, a two-handled
kalpis, depicts Sappho on a more common black-figure Greek vase.

In both red and the black depictions, she has long hair,
either in a bun or cascading double twists of breast-length curls.

Little is known about her for certain—although her now mostly
lost poetry was well known and much praised through antiquity.

Sappho's poet-friend Alcaeus remembers her thus:
"Violet-haired, pure, honey-smiling Sappho."

Philosophy of Language

"The object of philosophy is the logical clarification of thoughts.
Philosophy is not a theory but an activity. Philosophy should make clear
and delimit sharply the thoughts which otherwise are, as it were,
opaque and blurred."
　　　—Wittgenstein, from *Tractatus Logico-Philosophicus*

I am gazing out the bathroom skylight, opaque with snow.

I am fresh out of "can't say" but can't say when.

I am some days wearing un-ironed irony straight from the dryer.

I am become melancholy poured over pensive
　　　　ice cubes, a double shot.

I am an asterisk anus doodle, three days in a row now ***.

I am traipsing yesterday, yesterday, yesterday all day today.

I am shaving, shaving eternity's paranoid chin lies once again.

I am convinced that until-hell-freezes-over will never freeze over.

I am mashed clarification with gravely instead of
　　　　gravy over mashed cauliflower.

I am reading like hell Dante's *Inferno*,
　　　　sweltering in medieval theology.

I am the cold interior of unsightly shivering at life's
　　　　stoned lessons/lessens.

I am dust-unto-dust sucked up in the Hoover and it's
　　　　Jonah-fear in here/hear.

I am dim sum chicken feet crying the sky is falling,
　　　　falling feet per second.

I am gelatinous fatty content on aortic holiday,
　　　　missing my beets/beats.

I am a mottled barn cat stalking dark metaphors with
　　　　violet eyes, purring perhaps.

I am beverage traveling to festive over-indulgence on
　　　　hummingbird wings.

I am vowels slipping repeatedly between frIcAtIvE cOnsOnAnts.

I am dark matter in homonyms: pray/prey, dye/die,
　　　　lie/lye, balm/bomb, horde/hoard.

I am sleep on a fitted sheet of soiled pathos before being
      tossed into the bathos.
I am whenever at whatever time allover becomes
      overruled and overlooked.
I am sometimes a rollicking haiku laughing myself
      into senryu or tercet lune.
I am Van Allen's Belt taut/taught circling
      the mind's charged particles.
I am tautologies shifting in and out of whatevers easily
      as Eden's snake sheds truth.
I am blurred snow melting on the bathroom skylight
      flushing opaque Wittgenstein away.

Tohono O'odham: The Desert People

They lived in the Sonoran heart
gathering cholla buds
mesquite pods, prickly
pear cactus, saguaro.

When the desert lowlands
flash flooded, the arroyos filled
with brown water for their fields.
The tribe then farmed corn
tepary beans, and squash.

When the summer rains failed
they sometimes starved.

In an old photograph
taken by a white man,
an O'odham man and woman
stand beside their brush home,
near them a small dog
is scratching its ear,
their heads are slightly bowed,
and they are barefoot
with toes spread wide
on the desert sand.

The woman wears a borrowed
gingham dress with puffy sleeves.
The man wears a white shirt,
buttoned at the collar,
that hangs on his arms
as if it were burning him.

There were two photographs taken.
In the other one,
they were told to be naked.

The Truth About Storytelling

"Human beings need to organize the inchoate sensations amid which
we pass our days–pain, desire, pleasure, fear–into a story."
—Andrew Delbanco

irretrievably we tell ourselves stories

irretrievably as beaded water slides off our skin

irretrievably even as it makes our skin crawl

irretrievably if we make teeth-gnashing truth

irretrievably hope is a tightened heart noose

irretrievably we die, our beloveds will die as well, sometimes before

irretrievably aging, aging: often little wiser

irretrievably the purple wall of clematis drops its flowers

irretrievably some days Beelzebub drops flies in your coffee

irretrievably Agamemnon is splattered with Iphigenia's gore

irretrievably Clytemnestra prepares a bath for returning Agamemnon

irretrievably our house plants die from lack-of or over-watering

irretrievably St. George cannot kill those venom-dragons in his head

irretrievably we think we do our best—irretrievably, we usually do not

irretrievably we fall into black totalities of meaninglessness

irretrievably we will mess things up even more, more irretrievably:

without the telling of story we are irretrievably lost

III.

aubade

hang on now

to each other

twined in these satin
lavender sheets

sunrise splayed
outside our window

light already
leaking in

more laughter, still

dust motes flickering
in the growing light

Our Together Afternoon

"Here are flowers and here is wine"
　—Li Bo

Our lilt of laughter among wild flowers
and tallish swaying beryl-green grasses,

we sip wine, making eye-love,
inviting the extravagant summer sun

to warm and share our love gazing.
A light breeze pushing the two of us

closer together, languid on our spread
picnic blanket, the sun glinting off

our wine-sipped lips, inviting us as we lean
toward one another kissing lightly,

eyes open, intent on our pleasure-meeting
lips, joy exchanging joy. Soon we will

make love on the soft blanket, fully love possessed,
swaying trees blushing above us with shadowed glances,

their leaves fluttering in the slight breeze,
voyeurs at our together afternoon.

Hurry Here to Me

"Hurry. / What matters is to be / inside the prayer of your body."
    —Sandra Cisneros

Hurry here to me
under this quilt of Milky Way stars

where we will embrace the galaxy
of our dreams in one another's arms.

Hurry here to me. Under the star's
wide quilt we will warm away

the loneliness of you not here
beside me this sleepless moon-rise night.

Hurry here to me, so we may count
with laughter the countless stars of our dreams,

lose count of our caresses, so we are conjoined
here in worlds of that mystery called love.

The rising moon now says too: Hurry there to him,
your longing lover, enprayer your soft body with his.

Besotted

"Flower of sweet light / bring to my call your mouth of kisses."
—Pablo Neruda, from *Love Poems*

To be besotted with you is like licking the dripping edge of the blue
cheese dressing jar. No, being besotted with you is better than
any blue cheese dressing I have had on any salad. On life's salad.
But you get the drippy analogy. You are delicious. My lips finding
yours. Yours finding mine. I am bewitched-besotted as my fingers
run through your hair. Amazed-besotted you can drive away dark
nights in my soul. Healed-besotted from every part of you loving
me. If only these overly-besotted words could tell what my love-
drunk heart has sought to tell.

Love's conspiring

your eyes fixed on mine,
we are passion-blind to the moon's

indulgent light brushing
bodies rapt, entwined,

moans like a Perseid meteor shower
enlivening the room's dark

all distraction banished, we are
fiery as constellations,

Venus-encompassed, Eros-enflamed,
Cupid-wounded,

manically happy to be in this love

we two, heart-targeted,
arrows tipped with wild flame

Moonlit Night

*"When will we feel the moonlight dry our tears
leaning together on the windowsill."*
    —Du Fu

My love and I are watching the moon
apart tonight. Yet our thoughts yearn
under this luna-love reflecting light
for one another's caressing touch. Your
mist-soft hair is my finger's longing—
oh, when will we be crescent-moon leaning
together again, touching each other's heart?

I will say to you my heart

Where we go from here, Love,
is fate's ongoing slipstream

drawing us along, laughter-graced.
Your fingers laced between mine,

binding as rose petals to sepals,
we two unfolding together

in all love's practice. Your glances,
lava-hot kisses, saying more love to me

as my fingers brush your cheek.
Together heart-held in this presence:

all the eternal sighs lovers exchange,
those vows said to me from your heart.

Neck Kissing

Kissing you on either
side of your lovely neck

I am a starfish nibbling on corals
or a sea turtle grazing seagrass

that rises in gooseflesh shoals
as I nuzzle in, moans escaping

my lips eager along
this slope of warmth.

Hair brushed tenderly aside,
your throat moans back at me.

We turn to one another's lips,
fall into love's enrapt sea,

grazing still more on this yes.
Yes, yes, yes—

these whispers trail down
the length of your kissed neck.

Night's Quiet Light

". . . how can writing make it known?"
　　—Li Bo

Moonlight on our bed—I lift my head
to watch the spreading light caress

your moon-shining hair—faint breeze through
our open window ruffling cheek-fallen strands.

My hand reaches to stroke your
glowing hair—grateful for all the gift

of you here beside me—beyond
what any writing of it can tell.

Love being enough—more than even
this Venus-moon's approving blessing:

holding you here before me in the night's quiet light.

The streaming moon

"Autumn night at the open window / makes bed-curtains float and sway."
    —Anonymous 4th c. Chinese woman-poet

lights the bedroom through the half-open window
past breeze-ruffled bed curtains. Awake

and missing you breathing, curled here
beside me. Missing you this sleepless moon-sad night

as do all parted sleepless lovers forever in song
and poet laments. Their countless longings

like the mockingbird's mournful night-long song
frantic to throw off loneliness.

How can I quell my loneliness for you?
In this empty bed, you not here turning to me

here in this moonlight, arms meeting my embrace,
softer kisses than the breeze-floating curtains

as we turn to love's awakened sway. Come again
to me, again to such embracing, my Love.

Returned

Waking this July morning,
we touch love's order again.

Leaving last week's insufficiency,
we re-acquire our safe boundaries.

All afternoon will be our invited landscape,
giddy at the private scandal, twice

making love in the morning's early light
as though we had discovered

what no one else could ever know.
Laughing in one another's arms

because you are never too old for love.
It has been such a nice day, you will later say,

knowing beyond their surface the words,
relying on the nuances we contain.

saying desire

this dance we do love
of love—
no, of love's mazes
of skies spinning
blue to winter grays

quince flowers now in bloom
with spring forsythia sprays
yellow-yelling daffodils

but no, no . . . more this:
light refracting
through your filled wineglass

as objects love shaken or
heard chimes at four thirty a.m.
we hear, strain to listen for more

knowing love's drifting through
open windows . . .

You Come to Me in Tears

Tell me why
you're
crying.

> My day feels
> upended.
> *Sobs shake her voice.*

Helpless to comfort her—
holding her nonetheless . . .

> Do you
> have a hankie?

From
my back pocket—
Here you go.

> *Wiping her tears*
> *blowing her nose:*
> Thanks, I'll wash
> it later.

That's ok.
Are you better
now?

> Not really,
> still feeling
> crappy.

Really?
And with me
hugging you?

> Well,
> maybe
> a little better.

Watching You Brush Your Hair

"Your loosened hair which knows / no hesitation."
  —Raymond Carver

I am reminded of Goyo Hashiguchi's
woodblock print *Woman in blue combing
her hair*. Head slightly inclined, she is caught
in some distant thought as she runs the comb
through her thick black hair. Her left hand
cups the loosened dark waves away from her shoulder
as they tumble to her waist. Her comb half-way through
this practiced ritual. Perhaps her thoughts are of the lover
who visits her this night as she makes ready for him.
She is naked under her blue kimono after her bath.

As you make ready for me, brushing your honey-brown hair,
naked too under your blue robe, what thoughts
are passing through your mind as I watch nearby? Waiting
to touch your shining hair, to run my fingers down the curve of your
thigh. Have you smile, turning to me. My hands alive to your softness,
stroking your hair as we kiss. The *Woman in blue*'s lover watched too.

We, both, invited by the moon's in-slanting light. Knowing
the falling hair, with its attendant cravings grazing our cheeks,
entangling us in our lover's familiar embrace.

Your hair

a kissing tent
draping over my cheeks
I reach to stroke

cascading locks,
lips to your cheeks, your closed eyes,
fingers tracing the softness

of your ears
I whisper I love you
as you dip to kiss me again,

again your tresses
tumbling over my cheeks,
as we breathe in each other's

soothing breath—
sighing in our
kindled embrace

in this moment
love has brought me
your gentleness

Side by Each

"But at my back I always hear / Time's wingèd chariot hurrying near."
—Andrew Marvell, from *To His Coy Mistress*

When departed from one another,
only remembered kisses to sustain us,

laughter at missing one another
even a short few days—

knowing the return sweeter for the absence:
doves returned to the dovecote,

cooing in our love-nest.
Will we love each other forever

as in those endless love songs?
Not considering mortality's swift

undercutting of all love's declarations?
Yet we embrace what forevers

we have. So let us as in Marvell's coy
poem: *though we cannot make*

our sun / Stand still, yet we will make him run.

Title Index

First Line Index